AF225316

Monet, Cocteau Twins, Natural Wine

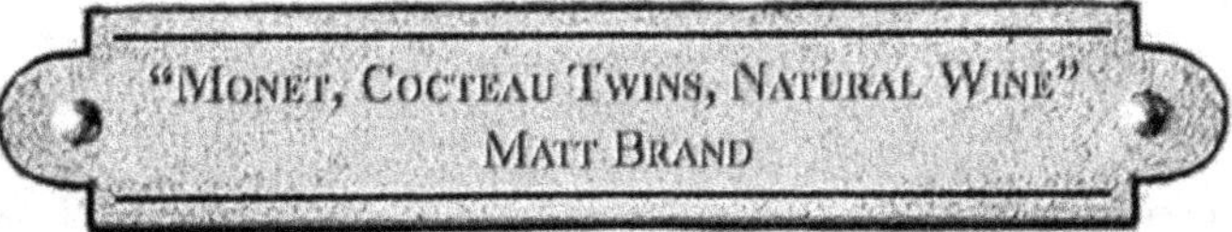# Qualitative Methods

Cover photograph copyright © 2021 by Matt Brand
Painting depicted in cover photograph copyright © 2021 by Matt Brand

The cover photograph's painting depicts an homaged rendition of the original album cover for Cocteau Twins' *Heaven Or Las Vegas*, as designed and executed by Paul West and Andy Rumball, released on 4AD in 1990

ISBN 978-1-953523-02-0

Published by Qualitative Methods LLC
www.qualitative-methods.com

First Edition

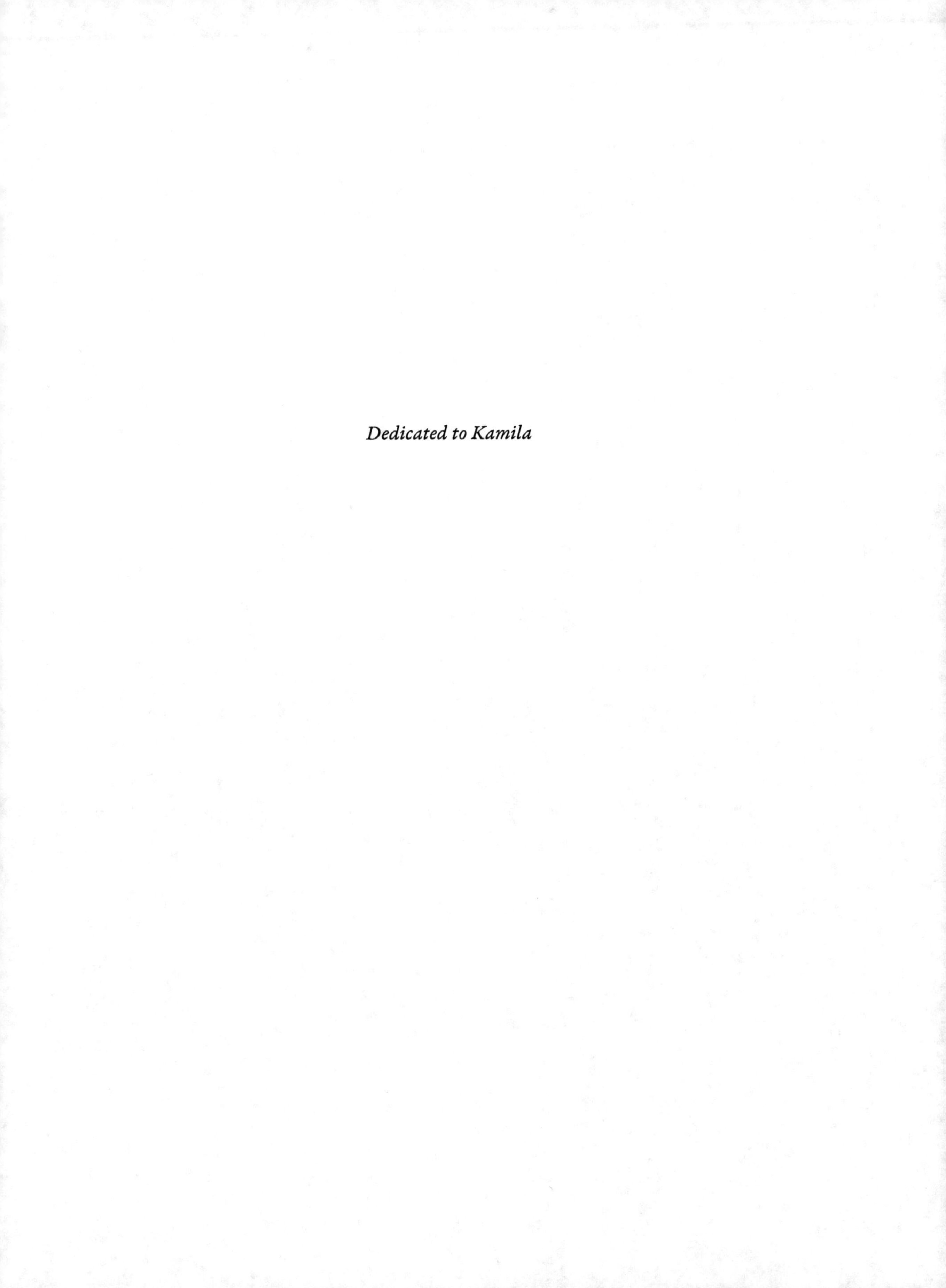

Dedicated to Kamila

Introduction

Technically, this book is the first that I'll have written entirely in Berlin, which would make it my first Europe book. Fittingly, all three references in the title tie to my associations with this continent, in one way or another. When I think of Monet, I think of taking French Art History at Université Stendhal 3 in Grenoble, of later seeing the artist's works up-close in Paris, months after said course, and now, of seeing even more of them at Museum Barberini's Impressionism exhibit today in Potsdam with my girlfriend, Kamila. When I think of the Cocteau Twins, I think of Scotland, I think of visiting Glasgow alone after an Islay trip with one of my best friends, Dino. I think of the C86 eruption in the UK, of early My Bloody Valentine, then of all the shoegaze and dream pop that evolved soon after. I think of 4AD. I think of countless memories of driving, flying, or training around and looking out the window, or of putting on *Heaven Or Las Vegas* or *Blue Bell Knoll* during or after dates, elated. I think of vulnerability, of love, of night-time, of neurotransmitters and wondrous novelty.

And with natural wine, I think of Berlin. I hadn't heard of natural wines until around 2018 or 2019 when they seemed to be picking up traction with a US market. I never felt impassioned to try them then, while still in California. Instead, they entered my life shortly after I got settled here in Berlin. I was missing the West

Coast's diverse variety of experimental craft beers and so decided to get back into wine instead, though I was craving something new and different. I perceived a culture of welcomed experimentation in natural wines, which struck me as similar to that of the craft beer scene that I was missing. It wasn't long after my first glass that I swan-dived into this new range of flavors and expressions.

Now, nearly two years later, natural wine reminds me of the friends, kind acquaintances, and friendly faces who I've met through the scene here—Ossi and crew of Motif in Kreuzkölln, Elisa of Rocket Wine in Mitte, Olaf of Mosto Wine in Kreuzkölln, Pablo of Naturales in Kreuzkölln, Emily of Ora in Kreuzberg, Jen of Rebel Rebel in Lisbon, Loïc of Senhor Uva in Lisbon, Kristyna of Prague's Veltlin, Philippe of Warsaw's La Cave Philippe de Givenchy. It reminds me of good bottles and memories with loved ones—friends visiting from the States before COVID, local Berlin friends, Kamila, a night with my sister at Motif during my family's first international trip, for the holidays. It reminds me of jazz, of funk, of punk, of experimental music, of boogie, Balearic, outsider-disco, and chill-out sets, of bender rave weekends in summer of 2019, of experimentation, of nature, of life. It reminds me of Czechia, of Slovenia, of Slovakia, of Austria, of France, of Italy, of Spain, of Georgia, of Germany, and of travel.

Monet, Cocteau Twins, natural wine—all three bring me to thoughts of Europe, that expansive landmass of rich history and complex geopolitics. I don't think I'm alone in my rather liberal free-associating to the continent here. For Americans, there exists practically a tradition of romanticizing Europe in one way or another, especially for the countless artists who often seem to yearn for some-thing within Europe and its history, something that might otherwise feel absent in the much younger and familiar United States. Perhaps for a portion of Americans, their romanticizations of Europe are attributable to some sort of subconscious guilt or inquisitiveness around what was left behind by their ancestry, a sort of desire for reclaimed heritage or identity. For others, perhaps it's tied to a similar curiosity about the European nations that had invaded, colonized, and enacted violence upon their own ancestries elsewhere in the world. And still, maybe for others, their romanticizations of Europe are simply due to an uncomplicated sense of wonder about the settings that birthed all of the artworks, conflicts, and cul-ture found in our formal education's textbooks. Personally, now looking at my own conceptualizations of Europe, I see that I readily associate it with things like self-discovery and inspiration, two ongoing through lines in my experiences here.

I first touched foot in the continent when studying abroad in Grenoble, France at the young age of 20, my first time outside of North America. The precipice of adulthood can be a funny time to get thrown into an alien culture, especially one outside of your mother tongue. At the start, you want to be self-reliant and communicative, to show who you are to people, to bond, make friends, and pursue romantic attraction, yet you lack the fluency and cultural nuance to easily do so. The resulting experiences of friction position a mirror back to one's preexisting personality and its assumptions, as travel and cultural assimilation so often tend to do. Yet, undergoing such an experience at that time in life, in particular, offers an additional degree of formative self-discovery—that being away from the familiar; all the daily challenges of communication and previously easy tasks, and the resulting confidence found in successfully executing them; the overall opportunity to morph through the integration of novel environments and cultural conditions, resulting in a version of oneself that perhaps wouldn't be possible back in one's homeland. To piece together yourself as you piece together an unfamiliar world can be both intoxicating and overwhelming, which, of course, also lends good fodder for reflection and creative expression. The quality of my writing from that time in my life may have been severely hit-or-miss, but nevertheless, the inspiration that brought it all forth was boundless.

The second time I visited Europe was half a decade later. After returning to the US and receiving a long taste of emergent adulthood, I had decided to piggyback vacation days off of a business trip so that I could go check out Berlin. There I hoped to obtain a gut feeling on the ground, to ascertain if I should save up money, quit a deadening career, and move to the city to finish some writing. Suffice to say, a gut feeling was indeed obtained. Now living in Berlin years later, I recognize how my time here has, in many ways, presented me with similar overtones of self-discovery and inspiration as those that I had experienced during my time in France. Of course, this all says more about my interactions with Europe than it does about Europe itself. Though, I suppose that's typically all we can really get at outside of history books and documentaries, just our smudged, personal impressions of environments and events.

In retrospect, both of my long-stays in Europe really could have taken place anywhere in the world. My initial time in France wasn't the result of some Europhilia or childhood dreams, but rather the consequence of university courses and circumstantial curiosity. Had I not been so bad at Spanish in high school, then I likely would not have taken the French classes to fulfill a humanities requisite in college, and therefore, perhaps would have never studied abroad and left North America at that age. Or maybe if I had instead taken Mandarin and studied abroad in China then I would now be writing a completely different book, with completely different associations, in a completely different continent. But for whatever reason, circumstances of time and environment have led me here, so I'll make do.

The idea behind this book first dawned on me today, October 5, 2020, in Potsdam's Museum Barberini. My girlfriend, Kamila, and I went to their rescheduled Impressionism exhibition, where I fell in love with the tableaus from the movement's stars all over again. About halfway through the exhibit, I kept thinking to myself: "Monet = Cocteau Twins", "Cocteau Twins = Monet". Since my early twenties, I've possessed a perhaps idiosyncratic preference for flawed texture over technical perfection, obscure quality over pristine sheen. This was perhaps most readily apparent in my musical tastes at the time. For example, the guitar playing of the Cocteau Twins' Robin Guthrie just struck me as much more enchanting, rich, and swallowing than, say, the sterile, highly technical playing of Yngwie Malmsteen or Herman Li—due respect. The former's playing seemed to provide more of an atmosphere to feel out, rather than a spectacle to ooh and aah at. It reminds me of a Resident Advisor interview with techno DJ, Blawan, where he mentioned his tendency to mix fast. He shared an anecdote about someone coming up to him during a live set and suggesting that he let the tracks breathe more. I believe that notion of breath, of letting things breathe, ties closely to my preference in the dichotomy that I'm suggesting here, between qualitative texture and virtuosic mastery. Breathing space can help something reveal more of its nature to its witnessers, by providing them with the time and space for reflection and deeper immersion. My growing preference for this quality has certainly laid hand to my likes and dislikes over time, gravitating me more towards spatial music like ambient and dub, towards more open visual arts like abstract expressionism or grainy street photography, and towards a travel style that prefers flâneurism and diving down streets on intuitive whims as opposed to tours and site-seeing.

In their best executions, both Monet and the Cocteau Twins, to me, share the common element of breathability. Yet I also find a commonality of Romanticism between them, in that they both draw attention to passing instances in time. Monet and the Impressionists do this by capturing nature in a way that highlights its ephemeral essence, its evanescent beauty. They achieve this both through their brushstrokes' loose, breathable suggestions of motion in place of Realism's tightness, as well as through utilizing contrasting colors to amplify a focus on changing atmospheric light. The Cocteaus achieve something similar through sonic means. The group's songs revolve around the surreal advents and departures of capricious, larger-than-life emotions. In this aspect, one could say their music is not entirely unlike Soul music. Both contain bursts of strong epiphanic emotions, and tend to toe the line between the secular and the spiritual. Soul music takes from its predecessor, Gospel, in its warm, call-and-response vocal structure, adapting lyrical sermons of devout faith into testimonies of a more romantic love and devotion. Whereas the Cocteaus perhaps move in the opposite direction, taking human emotional states, and then packaging them in a way that feels ethereal, soaring, and expansive. Soul brings the once heavenly down to the earthly, while the Cocteau Twins lift the earthly into the heavenly.

Despite Soul music and the Cocteau Twins' traversing of a similar line between heaven and earth, their sonic expressions could not be more different. Soul music is generally extroverted; it's courageous and proud of its Black identity and resolute declarations of the heart's convictions, announcing them both for the world and the intended romantic subjects of the songs' declarations to hear. Whereas the Cocteaus' music is more introverted; it's still processing and grappling with the heart's interior landscapes, filled with internal dialogue and self-inquisition in place of Soul's decidedness and courage. Soul typically puts forth a more bright, upbeat, and celebratory expression, while that of the Cocteaus' music tends to be more privately pensive, obscured and ruminative, spacious in reverby breathability. The hypnotic depth of Robin Guthrie's effects-drenched guitar playing, Simon's tiding synth atmospheres and hammocking up-front bass rhythms, Liz's simultaneously angelic and alien-sounding arias, trapezing and roller-coasting through the air at unusual velocities—to me it all sounds like how the flowing waters and reflecting light in Monet's tableaus look.

I believe both the Romanticism and breathability common between the works of Monet and the Cocteau Twins may also be found in natural wine and its enjoyment. More than other beverages, wine's medium highlights finite moments in time by taking exhaustive care to spotlight singular expressions of passing nature—the vines, the soil, the weather, the fermentation vessels, all in their unique, transitory instances. Just how high a degree of importance viticulture places upon this ephemerality is made abundantly clear through its explicit denotation of the vintage year on each bottle's label. Essentially, wine honors and catalogs finite moments in time, just like Monet and the Cocteau Twins. Yet natural wine in particular also offers something that non-natural wine avoids—increased breathability. By toning down or altogether omitting sulfites, the natural wine-making process leaves more room for expression, more open space for nature to do its thing. It's akin to how the Impressionists paint more loosely, or how the Cocteaus' ethereal backing tracks and stretched syllables open up more space for a conveyed emotion.

Of course, the celebration of breath and transience isn't limited to only the harvest and production of natural wine; it also extends to its consumption. I don't suspect I need to argue too much for wine drinking's focus on the breath. Colloquially, having a glass or two has become practically synonymous with relaxing or "taking a *breather*" at the end of the day. For additional proof of this analogy's prevalence, one need not look any further than the brutally typographed slogans geared towards the "wine mom" audience online, which position wine, or "mommy juice," as a reliable destresser for young mothers, relieving them from the turmoils of child-raising. As is the tradition in contemporary US culture, these slogans and memes have become shirts and novelty merchandise for purchase, so that one may wear or litter their consumer-identity proudly throughout their abode to tip people off that, yes, they enjoy drinking wine and might be developing functional alcoholism. Karl Marx famously declared, "Religion is the opiate of the masses," and a wine mom shirt from an Etsy store might reply, "Okay, but wine is the opiate of mom." Furthermore, some of these slogans even make crude analogies to wine-drinking as a substitute for yoga—uncoincidentally, another activity that draws focus to the breath and slowing down. In any case, moderate alcohol consumption, in general, can certainly provide some time and space for its imbiber to breathe—whether they be a mom, dad, or non-parent—due to its dialing down of the frontal lobe. Though only with wine does one regularly decant the inebriant prior to its consumption, essentially giving the wine some breath so that it can best provide the drinker the same in return.

As for natural wine consumption's celebration of ephemerality, I would argue that wine, more than all other types of alcoholic beverages, provides an opportunity to create and take note of unique instances of enjoyment due to its vast variety of expressions, each limited by time and quantity. It is of essence to the medium, whether it is made as a hobbyist or at a larger scale. With bottles or cans of beer, both the typical quantity required for a sitting and the mass-reproducibility of its recipe and package design makes it such that it becomes difficult to pinpoint drinking a specific brew with a singular moment or specific person (except perhaps in the case of certain commodity-fetishist corners of craft beer, limited in either production quantity and cadence—e.g. Russian River's *Pliny The Younger*—or regional availability—e.g. New Glarus's *Spotted Cow*). Similarly, with liquor and spirits, one tends to give pours from a mass-produced bottle's year-over-year fixed recipe to their friends and houseguests over countless occasions. In both beer and spirits' case, the consistency of recipe and the virtually unlimited supply creates a reliable loop, a blurring amalgamation of enjoying a brand with growing casts of drinking partners and settings. However, with a bottle of wine—unless one buys countless cases of a favorite vintage or only rotates between a small handful of options—it can offer an opportunity to celebrate the unique, to give a special associative-bookmark to an occasion's memory due to the vast variety of options on the market and the ever-changing yearly conditions that affect their recipes. For example, I can recall the precise details of having a 2018 *Jamón Jamón* from Rogue Wine with my friend Nathalie—where we were, what we talked about, and so forth—but I would not be able to pinpoint a singular memory or the same degree of detail with the consumption of a bottle of Flensburger Pilsener or a dram of Lagavulin 16. For this reason, I prefer trying out new bottles of natural wine with other people as it results in more memories and reminders of others in my life. Akin to the grapes' encapsulation of unique weather and soil conditions, the wine bottle takes on an encapsulation of a unique evening, with specific people, at a particular time in each of our lives. I find it creates a nice dialectic of passing instances in both the consumers and the consumed. Perhaps to a lesser degree, one could say the same about the capricious emotions expressed in the Cocteaus' songs being in dialogue with the fickle emotions of the listener, or the impressions of nature in Monet's tableaus creating a psychological impression with the museum-goers in passing—which brings me back to Museum Barberini today.

After taking our time with the exhibit, Kamila and I exited the museum and removed our COVID-masks. Apropos to the changing light in the Impressionists' tableaus, the sun outside of Barberini had begun setting. The atmosphere's tones were in rapid change as we proceeded to cross the Havel River to catch a train back to Berlin. The foliage along the Havel's banks and the sunburnt sky against its water appeared disorienting to me. It seemed that spending the afternoon staring so deeply into the Impressionists' brushstrokes had resulted in a subtle overlay on top of my periphery's contents.

After crossing the river, we boarded the RE1 to Alexanderplatz where we would switch trains to return to our respective homes. On the journey, we looked out the train window and admired how strange the sunset looked after the day's light rain. There appeared to be a peculiar gap in the orange of the horizon. It just stopped abruptly in a flat streak, yielding a light blue, then resuming the orange once more above it, like strips of sunset and non-sunset sky. I had never seen a sunset quite like that.

We parted ways at Alexanderplatz and I transferred to an S3. Somewhere along the S3's journey from Alexanderplatz to Warschauer Straße, the idea for this book fleshed itself out. My phone was dead, so I recited it in my mind, to commit it to memory as it continued to unfurl and reveal its details. *Monet = Cocteau Twins* became *Monet = Cocteau Twins = Natural Wine*. In homage to the three, I wanted to put together a text that aims to create a play on Impressionism's technique and tableaus, that aims to capture the ephemeral nature and mood of finite moments in a breathable, rough-around-the-edges way—and further, perhaps something that could serve to analyze both the opportunities and glaring limits of the glorification of subjectivity, common in all three expressions. If ASCII-art is to Realism, then this book would be to Impressionism. It would be loose but less varied in stroke and typography than, say, Mallarmé or concrete poetry.

After the S-Bahn arrived at Warschauer Straße I went to the Michelberger for an evening iced coffee and a pen and paper to write the idea down while it was still fresh and unraveling. Afterward, I returned home to type out this introduction on my laptop. The paper from the Michelberger reads:

05.10.20
book entitled: Monet, Cocteau Twins, Natural Wine

quasi-text version of impressionism; textural ASCII-art but full words; embrace repetition of a limited palette; then also break out of that (e.g. that for top of a piece, then more linear/orthodox in bottom half to show strength of feature/narrative). Can even do one that is a text cover of a Monet tableau + Cocteaus rendition + pét-nat rendition. Think also of that one tableau

*of his, in winter—limited to a handful of colors. Used only stroke-shapes to
delineate b/w sky/soil/trees.*

- title doubles nicely as a good sell, by compounding a filtering function
- idea started in exhibit as Monet = Cocteau Twins
- aim for 50-70 pieces
- each restricted to its page size
- write in InDesign
- horizontal to mimic tableaus?

<u>*rules*</u>
- spatial not temporal; captures an instant
- emotive + nature; avoid modernity/industrial/economic focus
- some real life instances/memories
- mimic/cover other pieces (photos, paintings, etc.)
- must take up full pages
- okay to break rule a few times
- practice restriction (limited amount of utilized words per page)

*dedicate to K; french art history teacher in camo pants; roommate who
first intro'd cocteaus to me in 2010.*

I have since added one other rule: I will write and edit each piece in one sitting, akin to the Impressionists' employment of painting *alla prima*, wet on wet. Except instead of *en plein air* it will have to be in the stale air of my apartment during Berlin's current winter lockdown.

I suppose with all of this, it is certainly possible that I'm just forcing a seductively eloquent connection. Maybe I just really like Monet and the Cocteau Twins and have been drinking my fair share of natural wine over the past two years. Perhaps this may all just come off as some sort of petit-bourgeois or champagne-socialist (pét-nat precariat?) joie de vivre fluff from someone trying to still enjoy aesthetic and epicurean pleasures during a time of otherwise pervasive, dismal exhaust. But in any case, the *mono no aware*—the *lacrimae rerum*, the ascension of *Gemeinschaftsgefühl* into *cosmic feeling*—is all there, all here. Take it for what it is: a reflection on the reflections; changing light in moving water.

ix

Attention is the natural prayer of the soul.

—Nicolas Malebranche

Music is using sound to organize emotions in time.

—Krystian Zimerman

Wine is sunlight, held together by water.

—Galileo Galilei

on a vacation,   oriented around a view and   the disorienting
aspect   on a rooftop together angled towards the bridge
at a sunset there in one city or another, it all melts
and blurs, in a braintime residue anyway,   neither better
nor worse in a shared pastel smear for recollection   —
  still lifes, tree-lined bokeh, love eyes in fanning light.
up here a usual sunset has unusual clothes again and dares us,
  so we walk out of the underwhelm of the world's artificial cinema,
  the truer parting light bouncing still off the clouds and river there,
us in the perspective, here, looking back towards it as others before,
   as a better meterstick for time together,
still constant and   reminding of change
  all the while;
  feeding local flora and skin in the day, then handing it over to trust in the
  arriving night, that bridge to the other side of the river
      below, now illuminated,
meanwhile us, in a corner composition, up high, with origin eyes again, time away
  to ourselves inside the bottle of wine, like an elaborately decorated ship,
   unnoticed and beautiful behind stacks of wondrous used books
and last decade's forgotten, noisy garments,
   in an underrated second-hand store below a big red calendar

PRAGUE II

water is less of a horror movie when confined in a garden.
                    its overbearing wonder is slumped like a buffalo's head trophy;
            the indecipherable end-point of blue is made comfortable by an upholsterer;
    the seafood restaurant's supply chain's dance into a better aimed future
                                        is stopped by a noise complaint.

what a trade deal for all those lilies, every day with only minute change;
            underbellies hiding heart and lingerie, but this side,
                    a worse selling mirror, well designed but painful.

        and after so much weeping who can blame the willow branch for reaching;
                the same canvas so many times
                        ultimately gas-stations any tube out of paint anyway.
but that's the fractal of it—
            a hand of the scene, that can satisfy the calculus of being
                    both zoomed in and out upon,
like the dreams of the leather jacketed short-reading punks of the 80s;
                it was less about what was in the scene, and more about what it
would echo off of the back of the brain's interior wall, for absorption over time.

WATERLILIES AND REFLECTIONS OF A WILLOW TREE

pillow sheet sky, light blue like an infant's space
                and it felt like that, that being at peace in a warm body of water again
except here friends like a mental set, bobbing all around me,
                in late summer's buoyancy,   light from the cloudless day
        and the wine in the modest rented boat, shared with the captain and his sons.
                we all jumped off, south of Monopoli,
splashing sun flecks on the calm glass, like whiteout covering the darker blues
        so we could write something over it for awhile, turning the frontal lobe down.
yesterday was a head of orange, today rose and turquoise laughing out colored
        streamer paper ideas; dolce farniente vacation, the first we all went on together
in the middle of our lives and their risks in motion.
                        drunken back-floating when loved ones are near
is one of the rare times when i think maybe there's still a big, benevolent warm gust.
        normally i never have the time or the temperature's wrong, but here i am,
in the middle of so much blue, with other specks i love floating around me.
        like a lot of things, it required others for compositional reference and synergy.

        this painting is not unlike other paintings, in that they all exist together
        to add to the same point; a resulting secondary point
however, is that there are no tableaus depicting a lone golden success
        on the side of his or her private yacht, in the same such ecstasy as ours that day.

BRIEFLY MOTIONLESS WATER IN AN EARLIER WORLD
WITH FRIENDS

snow soft   snow soft   snow   soft   snow   soft   snow
      soft   snow   soft   snow   soft   snow   soft   snow   soft
snow   soft   snow   soft   snow   soft snow   soft   snow soft

wall window frame window pane window frame window pane window frame wall
lock latch
wall window frame window pane window frame window pane window frame wall
   curtain   sill sill sill sill sill lock latch sill sill sill sill sill   curtain
               heater unit heater unit heater unit heater unit

thought...   quiet,   calm   slower space,   private and home
       thought...   future,   uncertainty,   concern, stress—
                                        breath.   return to the snow.

   music respires   floating feathers   into the living room air

ambient   chill-out   neoclassical   field recordings

                                        phone off and away in the other room.
       stacks of books to read all over the coffee table,   the floor,
       advertisements for motion and preoccupation—   instead looking out the
window frame: silent covid tundra,   soft, quiet snow

couch pillow couch blanket pillow me couch pillow couch couch   houseplant

Passing Berlin Snow That Won't Gather Enough To Stick

the rapid sight of the   now empty lot
                                                 where Griessmühle used to be

zooming by the window while on the Ringbahn.
it takes a minute to process it, that Christmas day,
on the way to a friend's friend's apartment
for Korean cuisine and beers so that we three
ex-pats don't feel so alone. i turned back to confirm,
and saw the unmistakable graffiti across the canal
that i remembered always making sheep's eyes at
when stepping out for a breather at unholy hours
of nonstop weekends that never ran out of tracks
and options. all the canal bank heart-to-hearts and
epiphanies, back to dirt. i recall the sunlight feeling
like a warden or enemy to ignore back then, but now
view it more as breakfast, reading in bed, time with
others in new light.   the more intense bonding then,
varying in degree of earnestness, yet always needed
and productive, to wash the next track, to get out of
locked grooves. now the empty lot made all of it
realer, as it instilled this sense of responsibility, now
to recall and to pass-on as a way to verify, a way
to hibernate the expired physical realm in another
hauntological psychic cocoon. all a reminder
of the more important antithesis that physical spaces
ultimately invite in their ephemerally held area.
                                                 every nest's hollow:

TRANSIENT WINDOW OF PERMANENT ABSENCE

leaving rain   parting branches revealing the river shore ahead
        opening blue above   popping the pét-nat in Łazienki Park

we sit together on the bench in this particular spot because you wanted
to show me the Palace on the Isle, left of us as we face east, the water scene
in oils and light ahead, with two plastic cups and not a care in the world.

you need sun more than some plants i've known, and my brain starves for new input
so we went to Warszawa for the weekend- a birthday gift from you, delayed by covid.
the time away felt needed; us time, together in our element, in travel's created world.
you translating for me, me planning and arranging the restaurants, bars, and cafes.
back in our mobile bubble traversing a larger one, after Berlin's springtime lockdown

two gondolas, one bright green, the other bright red, in rotation before us
taking pairs of tourists form the steps to somewhere further out of frame
in rhythm with our refilling cups of wine, taking it in, in all smiles
until the impetus of having to find a restroom would move
us to a new location together, bargaining the night

ASTROLABE DE CANTALAUZE FROM PHILIPPE DE GIVENCHY

—thick silence or a noise's echo from outside or in the stairwell

stillness   ceiling   stillness   ceiling   stillness   ceiling

death being given a perturbing closeness   floating dread
unusual doubt   magnified dismay   unfitting rumination
          unease   worry   concern—

turning to the other side and adjusting pillow positions.

death being given a perturbing closeness   floating dread
unusual doubt   magnified dismay   —

turning to the other side and adjusting pillow positions.

remembering that the brain is in the middle of washing the emotional system clean
                    contour of wardrobe   contour of laundry hamper

                    lying awake, trying to fall back asleep
nightstand clock contour   pillows bed bed bed bed bed bed bed   vague space

RECENT DISRUPTED SLEEP BRAIN STATE

peaceful distant silence extending further inward
towards more farmland and distilleries

greenest green in fruitful indifference on both sides, rolling plots, sparse dwellings

two benign foreign cells on the bike path vein of the Scottish island
mouths and brains full of warm moss water mist,
vibrating in shared amusement and observation, gratitude flowing through novelty
integrating with the land and its water cycles

greenest green in fruitful indifference on both sides, rolling plots, sparse dwellings

inquisitive ewes, texels and cheviots, perplexed on their own trip
like the KLF album cover past the hand-laid stone wall,
before the lagoon shores, where realities mailbox from back home

waters of a different intrigue, alien stoicism, in exchanges of polarities, yet keeping
to itself and those floating in observation

Jura all the while, even more offshore, majestic in distance, still, in organic proximity

PASTORAL EVENING WALK ALONG ISLAY

my aging, used car with its headlights off, resting in a strangely pleasant glow
in front of the strip mall's suburban frozen yogurt chain and japanese supermarket.
decompressing back in the world after our drive to the lookout point above town,
a hot air balloon touching back down after trusted climbs, fun unpredictable turns,
and cosmic nature formations feeling otherworldly for being so near to our homes.
it's night now, after lanterned skies of comatosing gradients, tangerine, turquoise,
indigo, denim pairs of legs in the two front seats, torsos turned, innocently kissing,
parked in an age where that already felt endangered. the engine off and
an aux-cord rivered between a cassette-adapter and an outdated ipod playing heaven
or las vegas; which one was still unclear. by that i mean, i had a freshly cut mohawk,
just because, in this moment i forget why
we had to go back to respective colleges in a matter of weeks, in any case. still,
maybe that's why i had to turn the volume knob up
because the reprieve of fraser's flowing trapeze perfectly hung like a car, tenderly
taking camelback hills on a thrilled, fast yet careful
ascent or   descent, before or   after   the summer sunset
light. those levitating vocals, now draping sheets against the windshield, tenting
indifference towards the teenagers and families licking their melting frozen yogurts;
while we privately iglooed in that warm awake-nap feeling, making out
to wolf in the breast,   perpetual, how true and real,   in the song's somersaults,
there in the vehicle's created space.   before our unlacing into separate cars
that would vapor trail back to our parents' houses,
in unfortunately opposite directions

A Song's Length In Strip Mall Signs' Light After A Sunset

san andreas fault silhouette like a vague relative in a faded family photo's background
submerged in night's ocean color, hiding the pacific beyond it,
               on this side the netted stars, like escaped plankton under the microscope,
always depicted as stationary or steadfast, but here they're buzzing fuzzy contours,
                                        oil paints or a hum

highway 280 itself passing in blurs between nature and undefined anonymous spaces
            my adolescent head slung like a dog's out the window, gawking up as i drove.

                all of it, stationary and steadfast, from this early tableau,
          so novel and inspirational, i mean to say
how could one ever forget it, this, or later; ever
          in such intensity, coming down from coffees, made sensitive to better feel it
late at night with the heater blasting and the car stereo orchestrating the sparkling
          to enhance it at this speed, back then before the region harvested flood lights
                and fake-cars, unaffordable rent prices for the late night cafés;
                        all before i left for a different view on the old buzzing fuzz

now gawking back up at it, i must have painted this a hundred times in those years;
yet night colors never paled in each instance, the contents never stopped humming;
          all obscure and direct at unknown velocity, so light could reach a future reception

Driving Home From A Favorite Late Night Café At 20

the other side, left,
                    its well foot-trafficked churches and the sturdy Villa della Regina.

moving water between us, from somewhere, to somewhere else, as it does
                              outside of travel blogs, quietly minding all its own

Sean and I meandering down the bank of the Italian river
                                                    in night's calm mystery
like a faint foreign soap opera on late night rerun,
                                          itself banking something similar.
snapping street photos, motioning in small sips
                                  of imported Brooklyn Brewery IPAs
through our progressing bodies in trade, out of disposable cups,

              which i now recall from an even stranger side of the river, years later

FLÂNEURING PO RIVER TOWARDS PARCO DEL VALENTINO;
APPRAISAL FOR OVERLOOKED, NATURAL SITES

the underrated joy of walking away from the sound

                    of friends or recently acquainted fellow travelers,
                    around food or fire, the communal motifs with
                    a crackle of energy and magical air like a cauldron spell

to a position far enough away
          where wilderness ambiance fills more air than the faint relating behind you
          where the neutral night-shadow cradles invitingly like a familiar memory

relieving yourself and taking the opportunity to ogle up like a newborn creature,
          either during or after, to remember the during-and-afterness, of what's ahead.

          so many small, stupifying hidden churches all abound in these away places,
          always offering this private opportunity; sliding you the old library book
          for another renewal before the due date. you quietly read an old passage.

then the returning back to the powwow, not feeling a need to remark upon any of it,
                    as it so often is, with private matters or the obvious

NATURE CALLS

well, given the view
                    that it is, after all,
                                    all natural, all the same matter,

            then you sipping that afternoon negroni, that aperitivo, that beer in the sun,
                what a grandparent, what a umarell, what a leisurely history buff,
                    the father, the son, the holy ghost in this country or any other,
                        placed in it, the historic materialism over time—right, and

that brings me back to the intoxicated point to be erected here,
            high off our own achievements or maybe just enthusiastic to relate the same
                further along—as i was saying,

historically in that moment, from your seat observing the piazza's fountain or statue
            honoring this old technology that we spectacularize; moving it further along
                in reductions back into earth stuff, a corroding stone carving,
                        a rusting metal placard, a textbook caption, a video clip
                            detailing that it's all just advancements
                                        in whatever helps the messages sustain
                                            further over time, through us

why is there never one for laughter, never a just stone bust reading: hahahahaha
    you might think, smiling self-satisfied with the last of the drink and brittle bones
        before standing, to go seal back in, to one type of work or another

IMPROVING UPON BRONZE AND MARBLE

i prefer being alone-but-not-alone, most notably on my birthday.
        one year i took the day off and went to the beach,
            staring out at the big water and then having an iced coffee, "maybe, because,"
            that combination feels right together, as a description of a birthday.

this time i decided to go further away for the same, a soft isolation
            to better see from a distance,
            like how floating collections of gas are connected with invisible lines
            to receive their names and likeness to animals or mythologized fantasies.

so i bought a discounted last-minute ticket to tokyo. the day aligned perfectly, there
            with the fall of cherry blossoms; it felt so alien and true, to be so far along
            the meguro river, in the middle of crowds of others participating in hanami,
            photographing themselves and the flowers in transience.

to further pattern the microcosm of it all, or whatever i'm in, i put on headphones
            introducing the deceased susumu yokota's *sakura* into the scene.
            i bought a pathside plastic flute of pink champagne with petals in it
            to commemorate the moment, joining in the hanami. happy to be alone and
            dying in a safe way from a distance, like a dog, a slowly leaking boat, or snow.

the champagne precipitated into warm globes, reflecting quiet photos of the petals
            in their calm pauses between gentle gusts, some painlessly falling
            into the river, others still only budding. and like a whisper, how strange,
            it happens all the time, every year.

i reverently used the public restroom between the river and the promenade. then
            upon exiting, i gave one last look at the whole scene, exactly as it was,
            trying desperately to make it permanent, a photo-negative upon the brain—
            closing my eyes, briefly opening them, then swiftly shutting them again.

BEAUTY IS THE EXPERIENCE OF WITNESSING THAT WHICH HAS
ALREADY DEPARTED UPON ARRIVAL

habits in representation,
>to not to be mistaken, there are shortcomings in these tableaus'
>allotted time frame; instance, insight, and finish line photos.
though nonetheless vital,
>all the practicing of the technique, repeating the same scene
>to improve, if not only to better see where light and horizons end.
it reminds me of Michael,
>a calmer friend of habit, whereas I, at first, was a surfer of impulse;
>a man of tradition, and I, of liberation;
>a believer and a skeptic walk into a bar.
>still, we negotiated our own code, a shared language, mutual values,
>as with any good companionship, over time.
friendships, like paintings, reveal themselves as another identity praxis of negation.
>guardrails around a watch; weekend plans, and syncing schedules,
>two hands, to help tell a more precise time after reading one another.
As a result, I've become better versed in letting the paint dry, seeing now how
>different mediums require different amounts of time, different
>strokes and applications for different subjects and occasions.
it happens all around us, as one such example,
>if I were to paint a fish in Monterey, I might name it Hume,
>and if it swam ordinarily, unperturbed, just below the bay windows
>every day, in observation and familiarity, then I would paint it
>with more detail, dark to light, thick over thin, in studious patience
>seeing it better with each return, each layer and flatbrush stroke,
under matter of fact sunlight, building steadfast off of suspended disbelief.

Where The Water Goes At Low Tide

birds peacefully bivouacking in the park's back bushes past new years
      waxwings and others coming from even colder situations to make due.
          since i go to bed too late, i'd both miss them and get called a bird
            by my lovebird in the early evenings when we huddle,
bringing home new and used pieces of language to place in each other's ideas,
     like tendril and fibril, lisle and scion,
         as a way to care and survive over small migratory migraines.

early this morning, still half-asleep, i get up to use the restroom and see, blurry-eyed,
     a bundle of regional slang, dictionary page ribbons, and terms of endearment,
     perched outside a new tenant's window, empty and gathering snow,
     like a lost winter collection of raymond chandler short stories back home.
i see it from the vantage of my own,
      in the kitchen with the lights off, and the sun not yet intruding,
       from between spatulas and stainless saucepans,
         past the vacation photos, love letters, and bills
           all tribally hung to the refrigerator,
  as i wondered how long it had been there, or if i just hadn't noticed until now

MORNING LARK IN TRIAL

                    not a single cloud in the cold sky
                              angled sun, eclipsing through
                                the current horizon, at the
                                end of my block

street's left side of Altbauen   street's right side of Altbauen

bare linden branches with   bare linden branches
melting two-day-old snow   with no more snow

Flo making coffees at the café,
emitting a heavenly ambient mix~

                    me standing in the middle
                  of the street aside the parked cars
              taking my mask off to feel the sun, closing my eyes
              then walking away afterward with a surreal turquoise-blue
          photo-filter afterimage as i walk back to the café, grinning

others walking down the sidewalk   someone looking for parking
knitted in smiles   filled with hope

LAST DAY OF JANUARY

                                                    atmosphere
              unique instance of light
                                                          faint, distant sound
                                    tiny whirlpooling thoughts
              a dream's residue
history   possibilities in consideration
                              skinned dam
                              approximating its
                              balance and desires
                              reperpetuating itself
                              gently in response
                              to and against
                    carbon's unstable licks of erosion;
                    conservation of energy seeking itself
                    in liked-minded oppositions to further
                    its experience of awareness, contributing
                    back to strange givens, wisps in exchange

REFLECTION AFTER A MORNING SHOWER

lucky enough to ever
meadow a smile twin

                    mirror dance a future night,
                    big and nimble,
                    circumstancing, round and swift
              reversing its echo from myth and bells
              catching unborn flowers in the air

       ring a ringing ring, sent backward to see,
ring it back in reels and dreams, you plea, you plea

                    slow-mo the home movies' ether glow,
                  all scenes in corks and soft swings boughed
            flight sounds made pretend in tinsel tease
            lightly flicking sounds in fluttered ease

          horses loping, in commercial's comedy cope,
          like a joke, you say it's true, i know it's true
worth all the days and silly sayings
to say it's true: it's true, you always knew

devotioning blueprints past played out pubs
for turtle-doving turtle doves, dovetailed in troughs
                  of tufts wafting light in sunnied laundry swirls
                  adieuing vintage wars and the lackluster burls

it's coming true, it's coming true
all the things you wish you knew,
the rings, the rain,
the song reverbing through

COVER OF "ELLA MEGALAST BURLS FOREVER"

birds nearly still
in the wind   subtly changing
                              train   landscape
                             pulling
                           itself away,
                          you must have
          passing   surely been on this
scenery gaining   over a hundred times   indifferent
   increasing   now in one way or another   trees
irrelevance   as so many others around you
                   and before you have, looking back
                  out the caboose window with drying
                sweat from barely making it to the station
              in time, the hangover or cheap coffee coating
            your mouth to encourage a swallow or ablutions to
          help you into your seat. What about reading a book or
        a walk to the dining car, texting knowns from beforehand,
      emails, work, a show or movie on the portable device, a puzzle,
    double-checking arrangements for where you're headed, anything
   aside from looking at the recent photos, best not to do that quite yet,
  instead quickly double-check that the luggage is still there, that this isn't
 like that one recurring dream where you go from wagon to wagon searching
for something unspecific that is already past, or you come to convince yourself
that you misread the ticket, or boarded off the wrong platform, suddenly seeing a
body as a negotiated representation split up between a growing list of liminal spaces

ITERATIONS IN A HALF-RELIGIOUS TRADE

                              it wasn't a postcard scene or even a frequent one,
              the recent bio-ambience had simmered most of those down into a sepia-gray
                       reduction sauce with floating chunks of blurry armchair pulp—

it was, nonetheless, one of my most memorable here. a local minor league
jersey hung; getting the call up... the late summer scene set with tracey thorn's voice
in a big identity-sized jar under the influence of an advanced digital padlock program
that i decided, after much trial and intuitive thought, to set to *repeat one.*

the whole living room was washed in a new honeyed light
after i set the windows free like a happy pet itching to run laps.
it welcomed the opening of the neighboring tribes' pickled year,
aerating noodling lines from below like determined vines
and the aroma of lovingly made pies in childhood cartoons;
the sounds of laughter between family members ballooned.
as unwed occupants across the courtyard played out the fun
classics and the hip promos to hors-d'oeuvre-tray more
open airs of the weekend weather, or else
coattail late afternoon returns from last night's extensions.

the whole healthy salad of it did the thing with tracey thorn's voice that
potential ideas do before they arrive
at the parking lot, or even suburban garage, of your attention.
i would notice it every so often, each piece politely giving frequency to the other,
in a way that still, somehow, paradoxically highlighted thorn's singing.

my head was the only part of me that would occasionally move
to look out that window and take in the memorable transitional light of it,
as if it were a movie poster (now it practically is, or the vhs box, the quotable scene).
as i was meanwhile maintaining newfound focus on a fresh painting i had started,
thinking about a coinciding romance formation and my nervous quiet excitement;
conserving more energy at the tail end of summer, to better integrate it.

TOP MOST FLOOR SUMMER INDOORS AT 29

an even deeper, still neutral darkness extending beyond vision in quiet construction
    darkness   lifeless, lonely gas giants dreaming of being pebbles   darkness
darkness   uncertain distance   darkness   a scarce cloud or two   darkness
    atmospheric pressure, greenhouse gases, atmospheric pressure, expelled waste

        evaporating disagreement rising like released helium, its decorations
    being forgotten   misinterpretation   escalated low legalese
terms of endearment in a trade bill   awoken associations   Sofia Coppola theses
    a buried thought of dying   a former partner or parent   car commercial
        children   freedoms   a made up place   incongruent math answers

streetlight   streetlight

a breath   elapsed play-suitcase of time   reapproaching the terraced jury
    clarifying the terms   softened voices   considered vantages and opened lenses
vegetables or tea   digestion   meeting in a prairie between two caves
        compound muscle returning to resting position after an extended stretch

        occasional passing car
                                        bicyclist returning home

streetlight   streetlight
            smoker

two-top   two-top   two-top   two-top
start of a purifying memory song breezing out through the speakers
                                                                        space-heater
            two-top   two-top   two-top
space-heater   waiter
two-top   two in physical bond, happily   two-top   two-top
            sighing into each other, as they
            order another glass of wine

DATE NIGHT, SUBLIMATING

rather better with the approximating nets of a caricaturist's try
than with photobooth laminates or engagement portraits.
 interrupting in the middle
        of a boardwalk's sick-sweet smell or a tourist square's cheap anonymity,
        the medium humbly asks a fleeting slow dance from a loose brick of time
     then sheepishly acquaints off its shoulder with   awkward small talk,
          unspecific embarrassments,   and loosely   sketched anecdotes, while
studied gestures meanwhile sing soft appraisals   to young carbon in movement
                                    from a remnant of carbon expired,
              honored and enthused in its tradition, an homaging cartography
              capturing oil and an instance of two metabolizing heraclituses
        in textures, uneven dust, and warm smears;
                        imprecise proximities and a limited palette to esteem
        the two, and whatever it is they were moving between then,
                like a sports arena and drinks somewhere,
                a child-free dinner and dancing at the hard rock,
                        a death in the family and refinancing a mortgage.

(at the reveal, the reception pantomimes the medium rather than an endless advert.
teasing laughter and blush throw a tent on the lot where a cold church would've been.
the charcoal elongates features through a portal of comedy that time's rigidness lacks,
    sticking a dime store trick-candle into the superbowl cake of judicial calendars.)

COTTON CANDY

less water lilies left giverny towards the end
            15 were destroyed by their messenger
                    who started making fewer and fewer.

                    all of them made you look
                                        down

    like here
                or here

                                        or here,
                                            next to here

reflecting a return down to nature itself,
            as later in life,
                    its silent-movie microscopic carnivals,
                        the repetition with subtle progress

    all with no edge or horizon, no docked boats, no people for reference

                                because it doesn't care, thankfully

CRITICS HATED THEM AND BLAMED HIS EYESIGHT

                    i had left the apartment to go for a walk, so as not to forget
                    my decaying body
                    and to treat the mind to some stimuli
but upon first stopping by the café on my street i noticed
        a suddenly growing puddle from under the awning,

ripples shattering its lone wine glass of held light,
like passing casts of senators through the long-exposure of a tv's glow

                    i sighed quietly to myself and said something in german
                    to the friend of a friend as we drank out coffees
                    from separate ends of the awning
        he said he's happy to be out for a bike ride, doesn't mind the rain.
        then he left shortly after.

i finished the warming cup, chatting with a friend working the slow café.
it felt nonetheless good, like checkout lines or video-calls,
as the amount of visiting senators meanwhile grew,
the wine glass shards practically filaments or static now, like a background.

we wished each other a good day, then
i opened my umbrella and decided to stroll, in any case.

WINTER LOCKDOWN

the time of late summer
                        when most flights are returns;
            and the remaining local sky, with everything underneath it, is
                    as impossibly colored as dreams' collective cinema.

we were all out at the pool towards the afternoon's end,
                surrounded by the region's steadfast olive groves in rows;
                alex, yves, jay, jess, and me, on our first trip together
                    transported from separate places.
        how long had it been, since we all worked at that one company;
        since we all endured and swallowed together,
                xylella fastidiosa and the subsequent smoke in the air,
        the neoliberal circumstance, the common conditions of atomized bondage.
                then maintaining our community, somehow, since
                surviving time, dynamic geography, and changing roles.
and now here, like an afterlife;
a brief recreational heaven.
                            vacation is beautiful like a painting in that way,
                    because both create their own temporal law
                    and phenomenological code, to which you
                    get to witness yourself and others interacting,
                like a spiritual ceremony or taking psychedelics together.
apulia's dolce farniente planted us in something of the sort that afternoon,
                with waves of balearic songs, chlorine and sunlight's harmonies,
            and the swaying incensed dance between laughter and endless wine bottles.
a new timezone.   no added sulfites; no deadlines.
        jay had helped me transport a pheasant's tears for the occasion
            its bright orange popped against yves's extended holiday tan,
            in concert with the pool and sky's jovial dialogue of sapphire and cerulean.
i held my tilted glass up to the latter so that their saturated hues could symphonize
    as i felt immersed under it, and a part of it, on a lounge chair next to my friends.

OLIVES AND ORANGES

i think lately of frost at giverny,
achieving the full picture with such a constricted palette.
relying instead on changes of motion to express, to exercise
matter out of itself, in a season when it's restricted—
molecules tightened in lattice, possibilities eliminated.

feeling   similar   now   in   berlin's   compressing   winter   lockdown,
a   shrunken   mental   palette   for   the   day's   possibilities
akin   to   food-scientists   going   to   work   at   yum!   brands   every   day,
endlessly   iterating   uphill   with   the   same,   limited   bulk-deal   ingredients:
cheese   pizza   with   no   sauce,   cheese   pizza   with   melted   cheese   on   the   crust,
double-stuffed-crust pizza, triple-stuffed-crust pizza, quadruple-stuffed-crust pizza—
feeling   trapped   under   the   snowball   effect   of   its   thick   coma,   from   time   to   time...
though on other days a new brush asks:

what   can we do
with   the   contained
rem ain ders — time,
att   ention, energy—in such
a way that sustains and observes, or what
might better result through necessity and return?
what hibernates below the years of brighter colors;
what might then arrive on a winter walk's
given distance,   between two selves in conversation,
(i c i),   observing dormant trees, before
the snow melts off of them, and the whole thing just
proceeds; what could be found, here, gathering
lightly, in the fewer strokes of the foreground

HOMAGE TO "LE GIVRE À GIVERNY" (1885)

off the bat i should note that they're rather disingenuous photos overall,

                    though we've already shared a lot of memories in their scenes—

floating, fishing, boating, summer posing. so we still clutch them close, fondly,

                              and watch: they're still changing, those tributaries,

still trickling out, leaving their glaciers and visiting our lands' deepening gorges

          through their afforded time. sure, it's hard to refute the silt's diminishing returns

but nonetheless, there come days where i can still find a warm-spot in an eddy
                                        like chairman's mittens,
                          or seeing a communal meander,
                    a looping, giggling brook.

        these remind me that not all of the photos' contents are stuck, that some things

still escape the nets and dams; like how no one owns those beautiful eddies,

                          eddies that are made, whirling
                a repetition against the current, a recollection sending
          a downstream fragment back upstream to repeat.
      freely pooling up, in a collective momentum
beyond its normally inferred position.

                            and then just as spontaneously, disappearing

organically, from the erosion, the continuing motions.
                              back under the current
to pop up again somewhere downstream, like a rhizome

PORTABLE POCKET-SIZED PHOTOS OF TRIBUTARIES

                                    such soft sweeps of snow swirling off gutters,
            s s   several stories suspended,
        s s
    s s s suggesting the scarcely seen shape of the evasive wind,
   s subtly silhouetted through
sheered silks and white veils

                                swiftly disappearing
                as dancing wisps,

slight brushstrokes between

        delicate powdered fingertips' descent

                                        all around, gently freckling

        fluttering flakes and angel feathers

in delicate detail
                            behind a fourth story apartment window
                            from an indoor warmth's contemplative,
                            studying eyes and moving mind, watching,
                            as shoegaze guitar sounds shimmer and swirl

                    sliding sideways pirouettes out in scintillations,
            syncing with the scene

flakes and angel feathers,
                all twirling,
                            flakes and angel feathers

Sunday Snow

unsent love letters to former cities

                                 sound

            film   souvenir

  ticket stubs

                         memory   epicenter

         paradigm event

                           emotion tattoos

  routine intersections

                                 background compression

        stewing phantasmagoria

     exiting through our warm fuzzy amps and grainy obsolescence

like a fountain, rippling under some unperturbed spring light at the Getty Villa,
or in Macarthur Park as featured in the scene from Drive,
or the William Mulholland Memorial one that I hardly paid attention to
while routinely passing by on commutes home from work.

maybe fondness, hypnosis, and the remarking upon exactitudes of nature
all paint the same, with improved depth through answered repetition,
perhaps, all reaching back towards the same degradation of the witness into
the minutiae, caught in a stupor of matter's persistence for return

JAMES BENNING'S "LOS" AND WINE SPUR A DOUBLE-SLIT

garden   group of people in august conversation   the elevated deck where wine
pathway   pleasantly forgettable   is sold and two glasses
                                 music floating   people   were lent to us
rosebed   laughing group in pink   queuing
rosebed   and white chairs   for wine   yuppy on a
rosebed   coworkers   cellphone
rosebed   at benches   encircled group caught in
rosebed   a debaucherous story   long shading historic growth
                 friends drinking   scattered pink   of healthy branches
                        at benches   and white chairs   from the unmistakable
            rosebed   benched group   of dates and   large tree, leaning in
            rosebed   echoing laughter   acquaintances   to witness and
                                                 another bench set   breathe the whole
                        rosebed   in relaxed topics   scene in
rosebed   rosebed   rosebed   a pair kissing
rosebed   rosebed   rosebed
                                                                              rosebed

rosebed   strolling couple
rosebed
rosebed   friends walking a bicycle
                                         through path   to the street
            freshly bloom-
            ing planterbox
            full of vibrant   bricks   shrubbery
            green growth   bricks plant life
                                                     bricks   shrubbery
                                                     bricks   flora
                                                     bricks   shrubbery
2 binary stars spooling into quiet orbit,   bricks bushes and small growth
    privately enthralled on a park bench   bricks   shrubbery
    sharing a wine that i brought for you   bricks   another tree, i think

FIRST DATE, ROSENGARTEN AM WEINBERG, 15.08.19

like 3d glasses,
   two overlapping scenes through contrasting color suggests a depth;
here motion; here light. a happening;
   it accordions the scene, pulling a cat's cradle taut, rainbowing a book's pages,
and that's where we always wake up standing—
   in neither primary nor complimentary; neither image nor afterimage.
we synthesize, into a world that brings us back to similar material, residually hanging
   in half motions; looping clips of dreams and memories shoring into distortion,
lapping tides swinging from starts and finishes to wear down a phantom space
   between their repeating travel; approaching the realer remainder,
itself, now taken as modeled form for live iphone photos, gifs, vines, tiktoks,
   all just evading the synthesis by reducing it crudely into naked thesis for grasp.
despite the precisely defined ends, the suggested space opens and connects
   on its own highway of latent material, all catacombs, sewers, neural networks
holding other ambiguities, other places partially or never visited. pooling
   the half-dreamt and the real, the experienced and the hyper-experienced,
which, themselves, lay temporary towards new end motions in softened matter.
   i suppose, that's where we're going with all of this,
      how the impressionists avoided using black.

ABSOLUTE MAP OF LATENT MATERIAL WATERWAYS

a placard's placard to the bored or simply curious adolescents and adults who recreationally took psychedelics in order to extract a monet painting from a local mall, a suburban parking lot, a walking path alongside the highways, the characterless sidewalks and model homes, a small manicured park reprieve between characterless sidewalks and model homes, parklets, the Nike outlet, the Walmart, a big empty lot behind a realtor's face on a picket sign, American Apparel, a skate spot, Kmart, behind the megachurch, the abandoned building, the big grocery store with the glum employees, the McDonald's, the Footlocker, a backyard, a stadium field, a nearby body of water, their bedroom. i can empathize and even find it to be practically expected in such scenery.

POINTILLISM

but everyone is good at it, or at the very worst, dormant or undernourished;
	the stirring water, the swaying grain, the breathing leaves,
	the cycling light, the passing clouds, the waning shade that
all of them painted, these are all soft things, malleable, early things.
	the artist dies, either prematurely as noted, or after leaving some work for it.
in either case, the whole lot of it ages and regresses back to motionlessness,
	back to classicism's exactitudes and hollowed precision—
	brittle in bone dust, cold in stone and stuck faces.
but the error breathes and yields; the open contains and bends;
	the outsider scampers away and recovers like a modest stray,
	on some bent, understood arc towards a stored final breath,
uncaring that it'll get, at best perhaps, stolen and immobilized for the same boring,
textbook end, the same instilled death trying to toll and spread to its opposite.

MORE OF A FEELING THING

i guess ultimately,
the allure, more the survival, of it all ties
to the moment's innocence or the impulsive candor—

avoiding the conceptual by staying more immediate to the event;
being faithful to the image or the emotion
by acting with it, prior to apprehension,
yielding an impenetrable marriage,
the type where a subsequent entity is seen as singular
because the gap between cause and event is so infinitesimal,
a history book's declarative, void of any clauses.

whereas divorcing the event breeds
cleverness's serpent,
lucre's considered whisper,
desire's strategy,
celebrity's pornography;
space to erase the actuality,
which longitude tends
to thread with and from.

what i mean is:
    fraser would improvise,
    monet would act like a camera,
    and us, we pour and let our conversations do as they need,
    in immediacy's paradoxically defined openness.

MOTIONING TOWARDS ARIES

the way they depict saint-lazare
        is the way certain
cocteau twins tracks still sound to me, beautifully and tragically
        remaining in visible reach, like an absolute of romance.

that is, the way they depict saint-lazare
        is an unrealistic afterlife, in its perpetual occurrence;
look at it for yourselves, and hopefully we can reach an objective point at least, at last.

i mean, how the train manifests through delicate veils of passing steam,
        is it not unlike the foretold gates emerging through the lit clouds,
before continuing to another platform? the eternally changing platforms...

is the endlessly concurrent moment of arrival and departure
        not the entirety to which we've all been either summoned or condemned?
and yet, one can't help but feel that it's defined in remaining out of true grasp
        aside from, perhaps, the moments of its observation—
        the zen of the painting, of the song, of the other, of the witnessing;
disappearing into the act itself
        helps one avoid an impression's pitfall of attaching
to solipsistic liberalism, identifying through insular experience as a delay or escape.

the impression's subjectivity brings the witness to either the heaven or the las vegas—
        the lasting beauty if it yields to larger connection,
        or the artifice if it merely begets modernity's lineage of optical liberalism;
        just as the wine offers a means to commune through singular instance
        or else the continued treadmill of commodity fetishism and distraction.

this perennial option of return takes me back to the gare metaphor. it reminds me of
the experiment about how if two people had to meet in New York City but cannot
communicate the time and place, then it is most probable that they'll expect the
other to meet in the middle of Grand Central Station's Main Concourse at noon.

MUTUALLY VERIFIABLE PHENOMENA

still, all the subjective attachments yield a nonetheless vital narrative,
the pervasive melancholy of a compiled history.
like, to continue off the last tableau in this series:
   the final beauty lies in both the cocteaus' and the impressionists' captured moment,
                    through the invisible lines of their spells' inferred joy;
             they both paint with color to imply finite rigid boundaries.

              they bring us to the precipice of possibility, the either/or,
                keeping the outcome hidden—suggested, but hidden.
                      it gives a double entendre to the las vegas,
   in that by filling us with a moment of elated excitement and overwhelming beauty
             we are subsequently provided a receding tide's whispers of fear,
                  the possibility of impending loss, the gamble of ends—
of the song, the moment, the described romance, the depicted nature, the stage of
modernity, the musicians' relationships, the museum visit, the conducive climate,
the fertile soil, the shared bottle, the present friendships, the paralleled velocities,
the novelty, the reveal.

                  the impressionist's scene shows the beauty of nature
                      if else the loss of it in the modern subjects in paris

          the witnessing of the beauty is contingent on both the awareness
                 and the forgetting of its subsequent risk of loss and absence.

          both the cocteaus and monet jar up the potential of their medium's
                              expected emotional delivery,
   in such an undiluted way that the aftermath, their depiction's outcome, is laid bare,
        like a natural wine bottle whose label says, "here's the joy before the hangover"

and if we can agree on that, or empathize with the experience of that outcome, then
it is equally effective and realistic in its depiction, with and despite our differences.

An Underpainting Of Unifying Suffering

there's a dangerous film,
or photo, or book, or song,
or commercial, or greeting card, or travel brochure,
...or was it a family photo, or a game show prize,
or just a bottle of wine—
well, a body of some assumed work's result in any case,

and it rhymes at an increasing rate, really a disturbingly increasing rate.
i remember just how often it is during disputes or at night, against the dark.
the rhyme may be whimsical and ubiquitous, but not benign,
like the old testament or sports fanaticism. it waxes and wanes tonally
in how it sounds, how beneficial or hindering its representation appears.
wet dreams or dead ends, fake beaches or impossible castles

i mean, okay—yes, it's beautiful. we should talk about this, yeah,
and still enjoy it; examine it rather than hide it. that is what is
critical here, how we all ought to bring it into the cold, honest light,
or into our party conversations, in their recession or refinement.

as anything, i guess the point is to take care and to question
it away into disintegrative realism and proper digestion,
through the body instead of the mind. through the ugly,
helpful prayer of awareness that always succeeds
in pouring its ice water on us through time.

otherwise, the rhyme stays on too long. and when it finally disappears,
if we're still around to hear it, everything registers as nonsense. grotesque,
betraying nonsense. it suggests that maybe we shouldn't roll our eyes away
at those who quickly point out the lowly piece's smudge and blemish, as
much as we should take heed of them, and zoom in on the fault even sooner,
in recognition,
since it's all we've actually got, anyway.

THE PERFECT MUSEUM

a location's   haphazard   impasto
made clear at some trivial moment
                like while inserting your mailing address for an online order.
the funny reverse whirlpool appears, like a microscopic mosaic of digital artifacts
                emerging rather psychedelically; a spiritual hand reaching down
                        through the contrasting weather and the land that it visits.

it takes a year or two to fully dry
        but then the composition reveals the truer nature of the space and its use.
        first the pushing of the paint somewhere or another and
                enduring the toil through a grim rental market and local conditions;
why this space
                                and not that one   or that one,
                what felt intuitively wrong about this other one?
        why didn't they choose you   but this one finally did?
so much strange, dormant power in street numbers,
                in varying positions towards the sun, or from the street noise.

returning... how desperation and turpentine cloud at the time of action;
        you make do with whatever medium is available for the duration.
                        but after the paint separates in the jar
it becomes ambivalently stunning.   who would you have been
                                if the brushstrokes fell differently,
all these friends, the romance, quotidian rituals, background images,
        how they each combined, and all the synthesized ideas that they sparked.

                        would it have birthed the same way with another?
you might inquire the light through the changing tree outside your kitchen window,
but neither would be any different, they don't care—not in a cold way, just as canvas.
        it's all painted on thick,   at random,   and yet
                        (it's pleasant to assume) certain.
that way at least, it creates deeper beds and hammocks, deeper actualized gratitudes.

PAINT WHERE YOU LIVE

i started holding on to empty bottles these last two years.
not in the obnoxious fraternity altar way,
but in the way that florent had, when we lived together.

he kept his above the refrigerator, some in boxes or sheaths
that he would take down every so often
when moving them to access a decanter,
recollecting the respective evenings in warm you-had-to-be-there brevity.
i'd like to think there's a bottle or two there now from our year of cohabitation,
when i first absorbed how to really appreciate wine.

i tried to contact him when i revisited that city, now nearly ten years gone
like the zeppelin album that we had listened to on repeat
on the sunny halcyon drive to the 2011 marché aux vins d'ampuis—
god, now i remember the montez that year, myrtilles et poivre... you had to be there.
he didn't reply to the message i sent to his perhaps dormant social media account,
but y'know, i kind of like it better that way; preserved in the bottle of that time,
and that's that.

as a consolation i bought a bottle of the local foothills' historic génépi
that we would drink with friends after memorable dinners,
as well as a bottle of bonal, which i had more recently discovered with friends in italy.
i took both back to my current home in berlin.

they're now empty, next to a growing collection of the past two years'
most memorable wine bottles, stood up quiet and unremarkable
on a counter above the washing machine,
illuminated by the window's passing seasonal light,
like some peculiar fraternité altar.

BONS SOUVENIRS

a reproduced piece of art's secondary aura,
itself, creates an aura
                with me now feeling more precious out of a third time and place
where i recollect the private exhibitions in a previous city, a previous era—
                now just a composite of exposures,
itself, a changing landscape's impression,
        never repeating,   with corners vignetting,
        contours expanding,   scenes switching and blending progressively,
not unlike the dream pop anthem from the city's past spirit,   years later,
        oscillating between fades and warm emotional pierce;
        yeah, "strange you never knew,"
        in the same place, even more years after them,
all updating encyclopedia editions, in self-spun nights or preserved hidings
        as maybe they had experienced, with those before or whatever lured them.
                and now pleasantly dumb, entranced on a different couch
                        diagnosing myself as a fetishist of moments,
        another secular cult of time, yielding backwards towards its shrines, and
still forwards as a hand to its painting, making new auras from secondhand ones;
                a strange metabolism of revisited modern exposures
        creating through a haphazard arrangement of mirrors, rotating in the night
when the present mind eases up a bit. like now, on replay, perry farrell looking so
high, grinning doll-eyed, like he's inside of the thing but also missing out on it;
looks so much like that city and its escaping mist.
        a place where there's an excess of time, so people tend to avert their eyes

JANE'S ADDICTION MUSIC VIDEO FROM EARLY
ADOLESCENCE, BEFORE LOS ANGELES

vital, non-luxurious cellars that seem to escape representation of color or tone, much
        too mute,   too dark, guarded,   even too liminal for this.
        what a   relief too, to   preserve in their own
        time,   blocking   off an arched space
        to   return   to you, later on ...
and all on its own, a natural bridge, or a tomb made by rainfall... like, consider the
oil painting and its quiet ask, to be forgotten in a dark place for about year at least,
so that you both might solidify in separate identity, putting a cork on light control.
it needs to be out of the sun and its bleaching aspects, though how strange that that
was the requisite at the start—to take it all out, into the truth for agreements in cre-
ation, prior to the need to stow it away, to let it quietly breathe and do its thing. but
what a great reminder, that even the light is just another character here,
under the same suspense that moves below and beyond it.

THE EVASION OF UNDERGROUND SETTINGS

in this current frame tracing back subsequent auras,
the first time i watched "los angeles plays itself" was on vimeo for free
before moving to the city, maybe as some way to condition myself for it.
the second time i had to pirate it, after the free version was removed for a remaster,
that was while i was living there, watching as a way to make sense and relate.
and now, i'm paying youtube to rent it, watching it off of a vpn in a different city,
los angeles still playing itself, it remains a favorite film to me, now in its glow at 4am.
i remember someone i dated there, we lived together for awhile
and that proximity revealed incongruencies, through time.
i saw her, years later, in london after she fulfilled her dream of moving there
i asked her how it felt, to be there,
and she played an existential bergman close-up, confiding that it just feels
like it's where she lives now; appearing to look back
to a former self, puzzled for having thought it would be anything otherwise.
as i continue rewatching the movie, i think of an old contemporary
artbook i had bought, "100 not so famous views of l.a." by a local painter at the time.
i leafed through its depictions attentively in my old apartment then and there, before
i grew familiar with its scenes, affirming the ones i knew of prior; it's all in a box now
and i'm in mine, in a different city of almost two years.
the aura will dissipate when this rewatch ends,
turning into something else, that's how it goes,
like how all the illuminated, impressioned places of france, still exist in the night,
outside of our view; undisturbed, unpainted. and then tomorrow
i'll get to discussing this film's lit scenes, the impressions, and memories
during a film-club call with friends, some who are back in los angeles again. i'll say:
it's still one of my favorite movies, even in what it lacks or chooses not to show

LOS ANGELES PROJECTS ITSELF

                    all it takes is a little sun
        to highlight the missing pieces,
                 the minute,   life-saving banalities
of the local environment,   all overlooked systems like
         plant life and   bacteria in their subtle, vital motions.
    the forgotten   spring smell is slowly opening,   a time's return
even at a social-distance now,   the fun, diverse city fauna begin congregating
back to the canals,   to the parks,   to the vantage points,
     as we stroll through like the painted flâneurs   it   opens up,
us   and the scene   in dialectic relationship.   all it took was highlighting
   the contrasts—   suffocating winter gray-blues
   with welcoming light creme yellows,   laughing tangerines, to make the water pop,
         to give the bare trees a sway and likeness   to ourselves and how
we've been seeing things.   small particles against the thawing city...
      we improvise the route back to our apartments as we saunter,
           in sudden agreement that we're in no rush.

and now, at home, looking back at it I see, how the route and our attention
were only guided by mundane points of nature and fellow, unremarkable faces,
                    all too easy to forget, as i close the windows.

BREADCRUMB TRAIL OF PAINT

inspired by it,   until and unto what
gathering smoke   dry living room air   sounding yesteryear records

overly enthused conversations   standard wardrobe affirmations

a numbing company echoing   a similarity of stitches   in comedy and agreement
delaying divine lonelinesses   uncertainty   avoidance of calmer routines

one person's quiet, rising awareness   another's nervous insistence
to continue   with those who stay   until there's no other option
one's desire to impulsively call an ex,   another's thought to text a taxi in order,
to stay longer   to remain in grasp
the abstraction of full immersion, of complete existence, lost to illusion's b-roll lens

the group   gathered   late   around   a   table   again
making something else do the difficult work, against mirrors
partially finished receptacles at various termination points
for each them,   independently in their head,   gathered in a contingent community

buried dormancies,   tomorrow in the bed or rude lobby light,   ignored mailboxes
inevitability   repetition's key
symptoms   a small rip   a final straw   reverse momentum
momentarily soothed with likenesses to art, music, drinks, novel products,
when does the new alarm clock arrive?   when does the old one get thrown out
or handed off to someone in proximity? when you're done with it,
what arrives after the scene?
one briefly wonders in the future, upon leaving a viewing and making plans for friday

THAT WHICH LEAVES

it's just a safe house or a halfway house here, in what's depicted
          there are windbreak trees, to show a movement and still offer you a privacy
in a floating halo around the sacred sponge,
          there's a mote of twinkling water, or a parameter of serene, dewy boulevards
outside of time, before our broken faces in gauzed gazes.
          the same wear is not visited upon these works,
our experience of visited violence
          is laid out of us through suspension, giving the illusion of absent time, hung
in the familiar space, in the museum's ambition towards a sterile afterlife.
          these anechoic chambers give us reprieved glimpses, moments still
textured, not entirely frictionless,
          of a view of past time made present, leaving
us still afterwards, to make do as we will, with that which arrives in the difference.

Bardo Light Adaptation Upon Exiting The Cinema

has every abattoir worker muttered "shucks..." upon waking?
i guess i only ask because i wanted to feel less bad
for any potential spoil that might leak from these pages, as i pet this last one
not necessarily sadly, nor even ambivalently, but just out of sight,
aware of the ever-present risks, like a parent or biology researcher
"good enough" or "it is what it is" are corks i use more and more, the longer i do this.
shucks...
i guess it's high time to stop flipping the record, time to clean the brushes,
to wash the wine glasses quietly in the kitchen after the party's left,
feeling somewhere vaguely between
a gratitude for what's transpired and a sigh towards culture's recycling systems.
kill is a strong word, but i guess i'm laying hand to killing something here.
the impressionists palliated the sun's terminal scenes, all matters of natural causes;
the cocteaus generously lent themselves as surrogates, contouring around the act;
and though the vintners use their feet, they still tend to dutifully end things with a
respect and care, perhaps from being the most in-control of the remains.

so then, what's the best way to integrate the light in this case...
to end it quickly would feel dramatic and coward, but that doesn't mean i ought to
draw it out or think about it too much, or else i might get sentimental. shucks...
maybe this is why some people always end up resorting to words,
to try to put it outside of themselves,
in a clumsy yet endearingly human way of imposing one's anxiety back onto nature
and others, like how someone at a funeral might say, "it's what they would've wanted,"
as an excuse that any naysayers would feel too tired or preoccupied to argue with.
i won't go that far, but maybe i can at least offer a few words on the topic,
like "good enough," or "shucks," helpful mediums for binding time until afterlives

MONET, COCTEAU TWINS, NATURAL WINE BECOMES A
WARHOL SCREENPRINT ON GIFT SHOP TOTE BAGS

ACKNOWLEDGMENTS

I'd like to thank the museums and museum workers of the world. Despite the persisting room for improvement in curation systems and practices, I have nevertheless received moving and memorable experiences from these institutions' displays and physical spaces, which clearly continue to inspire me to this day. I'd like to explicitly thank the Chichu Art Museum for housing the Monet water lilies and Museum Barberini for their rescheduled Impressionism exhibit between the lockdown periods this past year. To my beautiful, encouraging, and amazing partner Kamila for insisting that we go to that exhibition despite my initial jadedness. I love and am grateful for our mutual enjoyment of museum dates and natural wine, and that we can share so many great memories together.

To Maria Leon and in memory of the great Paul Milan, thank you both for expanding my horizons and enriching my life. To my parents for their support in my studying aboard. To the art history teacher at Université Stendhal Grenoble 3 who would always rock the paint-stained, blue camo pants, for educating us on French art and leading me to my eventual love and admiration for many of the greats, especially the Impressionists. To Claude Monet, as well as, Eugène Boudin, Pierre-Auguste Renoir, Alfred Sisley, Henri Le Sidaner, Henri-Edmond Cross, Berthe Morisot, Gustave Caillebotte, Camille Pissarro, Émile-Othon Friesz,

Gustave Loiseau, Alfred Dubois-Pillet, Armand Guillaumin, Paul Signac, Henry Moret, Paul Cézanne, Maurice de Vlaminck, Raoul Dufy, and the less famous practitioners within the movement's spheres as well.

To Elizabeth Fraser, Robin Guthrie, Simon Raymonde, and Will Heggie for their beautiful musical output, which continues to move me and enrich my memories to this day. To Ivo Watts-Russell for all of his work behind 4AD. To Paul West and Andy Rumball for their beautiful cover art for *Heaven Or Las Vegas*, my favorite album of the Twins' on most days. To Nicole Biagi for first introducing me to that album during a roommates' game night when we lived together in Seattle.

Many great bottles were shared with those dear to me since getting into natural wine. I'd like to first, again, acknowledge those who run and maintain the places and distribution arms that I've come to treasure in this industry, as well as a few who were kind and generous during vacations. This once again includes Ossi and crew of Motif in Kreuzkölln, Elisa of Rocket Wine in Mitte, Olaf of Mosto Wine in Kreuzkölln, Pablo of Naturales in Kreuzkölln, Emily of Ora in Kreuzberg, Jen of Rebel Rebel in Lisbon, Loïc of Senhor Uva in Lisbon, Kristyna of Prague's Veltlin, Philippe of Warsaw's La Cave Philippe de Givenchy. I would also like to include a thank you to the producers behind the most memorable bottles that I was lucky enough to have enjoyed over this same time period, notably—Marto, Petr Kočařík, Jaroslav Osička, J Novák, Dobra Vinice, Vina Herzanovi, Azienda Agricola Vittorio Bera & Figli, Jean-Yves Péron, Esencia Rural, Strekov Kasnyik, Lucy Margaux, Lammidia, Domaine Ligas, Weingut Weinreich, Weingut Heinrich, Domaine de Cantalauze, Pheasant's Tears, Matassa, Philippe Brand & Fils, and Weingut Schmitt. To the Michelberger Hotel for their wine festival two years ago, looking forward to the rescheduled follow-up. And to Adam, Jordan, Sam, and Josie for always serving up great glasses, top tunes, and lovely vibes in the lobby bar. Also an honorary shout-out to Jiri Sladek of Métaphore Beers; even though he does not produce natural wines, their spirit is very much alive in his work and reminded me of what led to my initial interest in natural wines, due to difficulty finding a wide selection of sour beers and similar experimental varietals upon arriving in Berlin. His beer, "Orange", is a bit of a love-letter to orange wines, and is among several of his productions that, in my opinion, beautifully blur the line between beer and natural wine. They remain some of my favorite beers to date, and come from a kind and true craftsman who seems admirably dedicated to a creative labor of love.

To the friends and loved ones who I've been lucky enough to share such bottles with in moments of celebration, therapeutic communal relaxation, bacchanalian revelry, or shared investigation. From memory this includes: Kamila Merchelska, Yves Laroque, Alex Doty, Paula, Jay Sethna, Jessica Zhang, Allen Danze, Sarah Jane Walcutt, Mareen Kowalski, Marc Willenberg, Anna Tehabsim, Mike Bulanti, Max Guillaume, Catherine Bostian, Sean Phillips, Nathalie Capello, Andy King, Valentin Hitorin, Laura Lange, Flo Schaumburg, Alexa Brand, David Brand, Mike Torchia, and Steve "Dino" Torchia. Cheers, prost, kanpai, salud, santé, saúde, slàinte, skål, na zdorovie, and gānbēi to good health and many more shared memories and noteworthy bottles to come.

Whether it's a different type of art, a different band or type of music, or a different communal practice such as eating or dancing, may we all at least take notice of these things that call our attention to life's unique, passing moments, the beauty therein, and the gratitude that such an awareness provides us. May we cherish our time with others and the laborious creative works that we are invited to both witness and to share with those beyond us. It is fun to collect and create our various impressions of preciously passing experiences, but, to echo Frank O'Hara's *Having A Coke With You*, if we fail to share those impressions with others, then I think we are missing out on something important and equally ephemeral in this grand experience of so-called life.

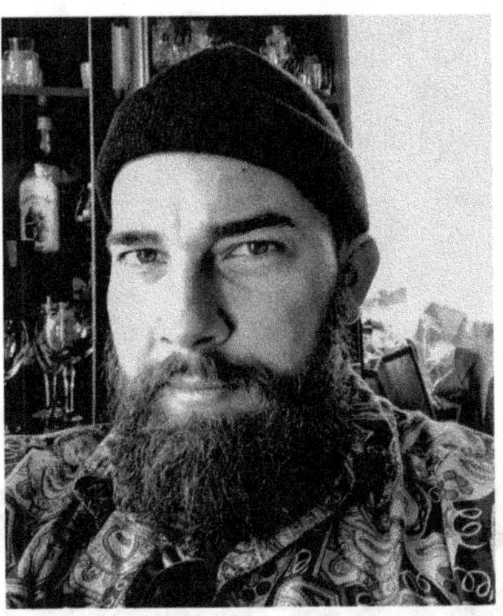

Monet, Cocteau Twins, Natural Wine is Matt Brand's third book. Originally from Redwood City, California, the author has spent his adult life in Seattle, Grenoble, Los Angeles, San Francisco, and Berlin. He prefers verbs over nouns, life-long amateurs over professionals, and face-to-face interactions over digital proxies. He believes that humans are inherently good despite our capacities to get misled or under-nurtured in our psychological development.

Matt's writing tends to orbit around hauntology and the human condition under late-capitalism via themes such as spectacle, intimacy, splintering individualism, isolation, and self-delusion. He hopes that putting such focuses on creative display might serve to aid others' reflection and self-awareness—to help comfort the afflicted and afflict the comfortable, as the saying goes. Currently, when not working on releases, Matt is trying to assess the best routes forward for contributing to sizable dual-power and material change. He is always open to connecting with others who are trying to do the same.

Qualitative Methods

www.qualitative-methods.com
@qualitative_methods